GROUNDCOVER
SERIES

Text research: Bernadette Sheehan

Acknowledgements

The photographer and publisher would like to thank Roger Pringle and
Sue Croxford of the Shakespeare Birthplace Trust, and Julie A. Timms of
Ragley Hall for their kind assistance in the preparation of this book.

Front cover picture: Hall's Croft
Back cover picture: Holy Trinity Church

Designed and produced by
Jarrold Publishing,
Whitefriars, Norwich,
NR3 1TR

All photographs © Jarrold
Publishing.

© 2001 Jarrold Publishing

ISBN 0-7117-1607-2

Printed in Belgium.

1/01

PUBLISHER'S NOTE
Variant and archaic spellings
have been retained in quoted
material, while the modern
spellings of place-names have
been used in headings.
The inclusion of a photograph in
this book does not necessarily
imply public access to the
building illustrated.

Shakespeare Country

NEIL JINKERSON

JARROLD
PUBLISHING

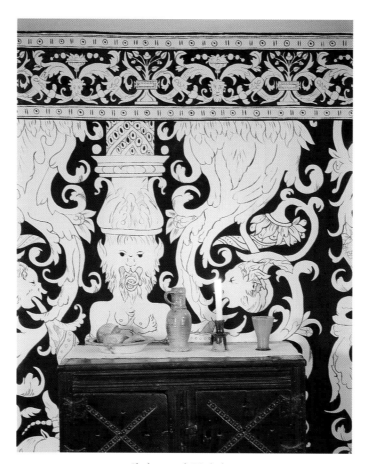

Shakespeare's Birthplace

Shakespeare Country

GROUNDCOVER
SERIES

The Royal Shakespeare Theatre

Contents

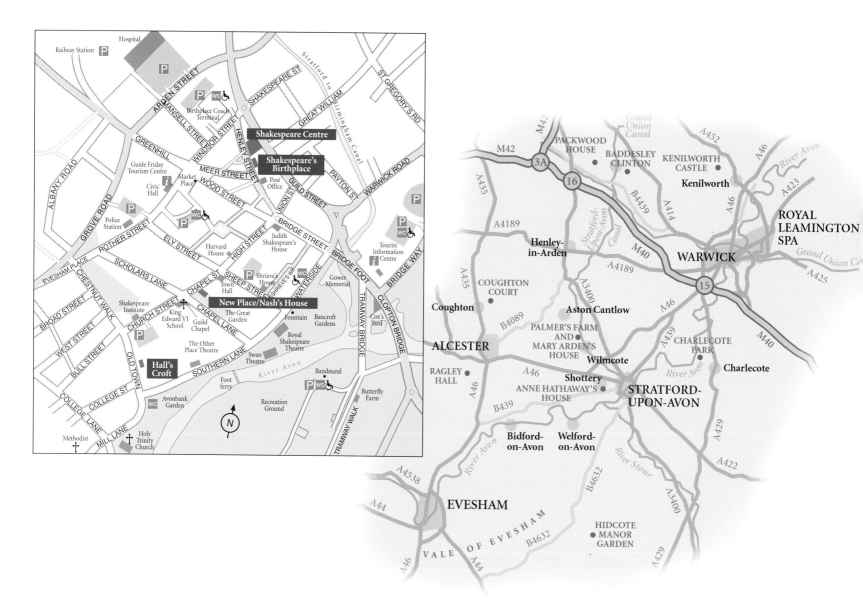

Introduction

As the birthplace of England's greatest poet and playwright, Stratford-upon-Avon has fascinated and delighted generations of visitors. Today Shakespeare's town remains as popular as ever while also maintaining a reputation as an international centre for cultural and academic activities.

Distinguished visitors to the town have included Sir Walter Scott, Thomas Carlyle and Isaac Watts who all scratched their names into the glass of the famous window at Shakespeare's Birthplace. The property was purchased as a national memorial in 1847.

Stratford's Guild Hall, Grammar School and other historic buildings have been carefully preserved and the layout and names of its main streets have changed little since medieval times. Wood Street, for example, recalls the days when the town was a thriving market centre for the surrounding countryside.

Much of this charming, rural part of England was once covered by the Forest of Arden – the romantic setting for *As You Like It*. The gently sloping green meadows, the banks of wild flowers, the leafy lanes, scattered hamlets and lazily meandering River Avon have a uniquely English beauty which is, perhaps, best appreciated in spring, as Shakespeare describes:

When daisies pied and violets blue
And lady-smocks all silver white
And cuckoo-buds of yellow hue
Do paint the meadows with delight.

LOVE'S LABOUR'S LOST

Despite its proximity to the industrial West Midlands, the landscape that Shakespeare knew has changed little since his day. The Forest of Arden may have diminished, but its oak timbers survive in many of the cottages in the area, including Palmer's Farm at Wilmcote. Aston Cantlow, the courting ground of Shakespeare's parents, John and Mary, and Shottery, where the poet wooed his own wife-to-be, Anne Hathaway, retain their romantic charm. On a grander scale, Kenilworth, immortalised by Sir Walter Scott's novel, is one of the outstanding ancient monuments of the area and was the scene of great pageantry in Tudor times. Elizabeth I was entertained here in 1575 by her favourite Robert Dudley, Earl of Leicester. The young Shakespeare may well have watched plays performed at Kenilworth Castle by troupes of travelling actors.

The photographs that follow reflect the timeless charm and tranquillity of the Shakespeare Country, recreating a journey through the very heart of England.

WOOD STREET

The buildings are timber,
and of reasonable quality.
The town belongs to the
Bishop of Worcester.
On Holy Rood Day,
14 September, each year
a great fair is held.

JOHN LELAND
John Leland's Itinerary
*c.*1540

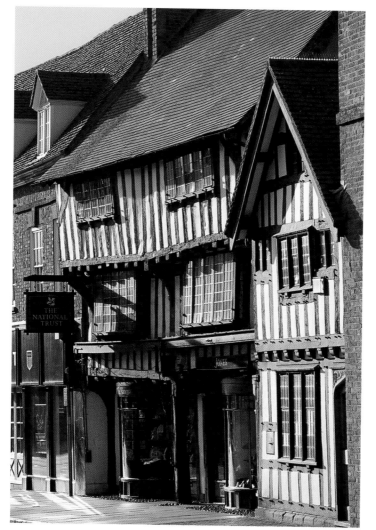

THE SHAKESPEARE CENTRE
HENLEY STREET

A very handsome job and highly
praiseworthy, because so entirely
uncompromising in so hallowed a spot.

NIKOLAUS PEVSNER AND ALEXANDRA WEDGWOOD
The Buildings of England: Warwickshire
1966

Soule of the Age!
The applause! Delight! the wonder of
  our stage!...
Thou art a Monument without a tomb,
And art alive still while thy Book doth
  live
And we have wits to read and praise to
  give.

From Ben Jonson's preface to the *First Folio edition
of Shakespeare's works*
1623

The Shakespeare Birthplace Trust

WILLIAM
SHAKESPEARE

*His Life
and Background*

AN EXHIBITION

STRATFORD-UPON-AVON
1564–1616

EXHIBITION

THE MARKET
CROSS

THE SHAKESPEARE CENTRE
HENLEY STREET

Containing His treacherous Plots against his brother Clarence: the pittiefull murther of his innocent nephews: his tyrannicall usurpation; with the whole course of his detested life, and most deserved death. As it hath beene lately Acted by the right honourable the Lord Chamberlaine his servants.

From the title page of *King Richard III* 1597

THE SHAKESPEARE CENTRE
HENLEY STREET

Stratford has been an important trading centre for centuries. It was granted the right to hold a weekly market in 1196, and was described as 'a proper little market town' by William Camden in 1586. The rise of the Guild of the Holy Cross from the thirteenth century until its suppression in 1547 also contributed to the town's prosperity, by fostering local crafts and industries.

SHAKESPEARE'S BIRTHPLACE

My first visit was to the house where Shakspeare was born, and where, according to tradition, he was brought up to his father's craft of wool-combing. It is a small mean-looking edifice of wood and plaster, a true nestling place of genius... the walls of its squalid chambers are covered with names and inscriptions in every language, by pilgrims of all nations, ranks and conditions, from the prince to the peasant; and present a simple, but striking instance of the spontaneous and universal homage of mankind to the great poet of nature.

WASHINGTON IRVING
The Sketch Book
1848

SHAKESPEARE'S BIRTHPLACE

The ceiling was entirely written over with names in pencil, by persons, I suppose, of all varieties of stature; so was every inch of the wall, into the obscurest nooks and corners; so was every pane of glass – and Walter Scott's name was said to be on one of the panes...

NATHANIEL HAWTHORNE
The English Notebooks
27 June 1855

[Shakespeare] was a handsome, well-shaped man: very good company, and of a very ready and pleasant smooth wit.

JOHN AUBREY
Aubrey's Brief Lives
1813

SHAKESPEARE'S BIRTHPLACE
THE REAR WING AND THE HALL

Like most middle-class homes of the period, Shakespeare's
Birthplace would have been comfortably furnished with a
wide range of different textiles including bed linen, curtains,
cushions, tableclothes, napkins and towels. The Shakespeare
Birthplace Trust undertook detailed research to discover the
type of cloth and dyestuffs used, and the Clothworkers'
Foundation sponsored the replication of textiles. Linen
cloths, stiffened and often garishly painted, were common as
wall-coverings.

SHAKESPEARE'S BIRTHPLACE
THE GLOVER'S WORKSHOP AND THE KITCHEN

As well as being a home, the house would also have included business premises. Shakespeare's father, John, was a glovemaker and wool dealer, and a glover's shop has been reconstructed. Glovemaking centres naturally grew up where there was a ready supply of deer and/or sheep, and Shakespeare's plays display a fair knowledge of the trade, including a reference to Slender's 'great round beard, like the glover's paring knife' in *The Merry Wives of Windsor*, and one to 'cheveril', kid glove leather, in *Twelfth Night*.

GOWER MEMORIAL
BANCROFT GARDENS

Hamlet's soliloquy, you know;
the most celebrated thing in
Shakespeare. Ah, it's sublime,
sublime! Always fetches the
house. I haven't got it in the book
– I've only got the one volume –
but I reckon I can piece it out
from memory. I'll just walk up
and down a minute, and see if I
can call it back from
recollection's vaults.

MARK TWAIN
The Adventures of Huckleberry Finn
1884

GOWER MEMORIAL

[Shakespeare] was the man who
of all modern, and perhaps
ancient poets, had the largest and
most comprehensive soul. All the
images of Nature were still
present to him, and he drew
them, not laboriously, but
luckily; when he describes any
thing, you more than see it, you
feel it too.

JOHN DRYDEN
Essay on the Dramatic Poetry of the Last Age
1672

CANAL BASIN

Most of the great worshippers at the Stratford shrine and the banks of the Avon content themselves with a visit or two or three of the surrounding villages which either evidence, speculation, or inference have associated with Shakespeare or his relatives. Comparatively few realise what a beautiful stream of its kind it is, what a wealth of architectural treasures – churches, manor-houses, and cottages – are distributed along its banks.

A.G. Bradley
The Rivers and Streams of England
1909

CANAL BASIN

Twenty-five miles long, the Stratford-upon-Avon Canal connects with the Worcester and Birmingham Canal at King's Norton and is joined to the Avon via a wide lock, restored in 1963.

HARVARD HOUSE

Ornately carved Harvard House dates from the late sixteenth century, when it was the home of Katherine Rogers. It was the bequest of her son, John Harvard, a contemporary and probable acquaintance of Shakespeare who emigrated to Massachusetts in 1637, which permitted the establishment of Harvard University in the USA. Harvard House was presented to the university in 1909.

HIGH STREET

Once Shakespeare is out of the way and once you can see Stratford out of season, you can still visualize the thriving Midland market town with the comfortable, staid, minor Georgian market town superimposed on it. In 1817 twenty-four coaches a day called at Stratford.

NIKOLAUS PEVSNER AND ALEXANDRA WEDGWOOD
The Buildings of England: Warwickshire
1966

TRAMWAY BRIDGE AND CLOPTON BRIDGE

...the navigation of this river Avon is an exceeding advantage to all this part of the country, and also to the commerce of the city of Bristol. For by this river they drive a very great trade for sugar, oil, wine, tobacco, iron, lead, and in a word, all heavy goods which are carried by water almost as far as Warwick; and in return the corn, and especially the cheese, is brought back from Gloucestershire and Warwickshire, to Bristol.

DANIEL DEFOE
A Tour through the Whole Island of Great Britain
1724-1726

BOATS ON RIVER AVON

The 'Stratford Avon', as usually entitled, deserves some fame even apart from its uncommon claim to notoriety; for all the rivers of its type and class, the reedy and the leisurely, it is surely the most beautiful.

A.G. BRADLEY
The Rivers and Streams of England
1909

CLOPTON BRIDGE

Hugh Clopton built the large, lavish bridge across the Avon at the east end of the town. It has fourteen large stone arches, and at the western end is a long stone causeway which now has a parapet on each side. Until Clopton's time there was only a poor wooden bridge with no causeway leading up to it. Consequently many poor people and others refused to visit Stratford when the Avon was in spate, or if they did come they had to risk their lives...

JOHN LELAND
John Leland's Itinerary
*c.*1540

CLOPTON BRIDGE

...such waters as these are for dreaming on in the full flush of summer, for catching the moods of summer skies, or doubling the splendour of autumn woods; for reflecting the ruddy glow of brick bridges, the moist and lichen-covered walls of old brick mills.

A. G. BRADLEY *The Rivers and Streams of England* 1909

THE ROYAL SHAKESPEARE THEATRE

… in its blocky brick shape and its playing with bricks as the chief decorative element – the one inspired by Holland, the other by North Germany [at the time of its building] it was a radical statement in England, very remarkable in a place of such strong and live traditions.

NIKOLAUS PEVSNER AND ALEXANDRA WEDGWOOD
The Buildings of England: Warwickshire
1966

SWANS ON RIVER AVON

Sweet swan of Avon, what a sight it were

To see thee in our waters yet appear

And make those flights upon the banks of Thames,

That did so take Eliza, and our James!

But stay, I see thee in the hemisphere

Advanced, and made a constellation there!

BEN JONSON *From 'To the Memory of My Beloved, the author Mr William Shakespeare: And What He Hath Left Us'* 1623

RIVER AVON

Flow on, silver Avon; in song ever
　　flow,
Be the swans on thy bosom still
　　whiter than snow,
Ever full be thy stream, like his
　　fame may it spread,
And the turf ever hallow'd which
　　pillow'd his head.

David Garrick's Ode, performed at the
Stratford Jubilee in 1769

SWAN THEATRE

I saw *Macbeth*, which though I
saw it lately, yet appears a most
excellent play in all respects, but
especially in divertisement,
though it be a deep tragedy.

Samuel Pepys
Diary
7 January 1667

FERRY ON RIVER AVON

Thrice happy River, on whose fertile Banks
The Laughing Daisies, and their Sister Tribes,
Violets, and Cuckoo-buds, and Lady-Smocks,
With conscious Pride, a brighter Dye disclose,
And tell us Shakespeare's Hand their Charms improved.

RICHARD JAGO *From 'Edge-Hill'* 1767

WATERSIDE

[The Bishop of Worcester] held and holds Stradforde. There are now 14^1/$_2$ hides. There is land for 31 ploughs. In the demesne are 3 ploughs; and 21 villeins with a priest and 7 borders have 28 ploughs. There is a mill worth 10 shillings and a thousand eels, and a meadow 5 furlongs long and 2 furlongs broad. [At the time of King Edward, 5 January 1066] and afterwards it was worth 100 shillings; now 25 pounds.

Extract from the Domesday Survey in
The Victoria History of the County of
Warwick
1908

WATERSIDE

The Steward of the Jubilee informs the company that at nine o'clock will be a public breakfast at the Town Hall. At eleven o'clock, a pageant (if the weather will permit) to proceed from the college to the amphitheatre where an ode (upon the dedicating a building and erecting a statue to the memory of Shakespeare) will be performed after which the pageant will return to the college. At four an ordinary for ladies and gentlemen. At eight, the fireworks. And at eleven o'clock the masquerade.

Handbill from the Stratford Jubilee, 1769

In the event, the procession was abandoned because of heavy rain. An ordinary was a meal at a fixed price and time in an inn.

DIRTY DUCK
WATERSIDE

There was a gentle tap at the door, and a pretty chambermaid, putting in her smiling face, inquired, with a hesitating air, whether I had rung. I understood it as a modest hint that it was time to retire … and putting the *Stratford Guidebook* under my arm, as a pillow companion, I went to bed, and dreamt all night of Shakspeare, the jubilee, and David Garrick.

WASHINGTON IRVING
The Sketch Book
1848

DIRTY DUCK
WATERSIDE

In the 1870s local brewer Charles Edward Flower donated land and launched a fund to build a permanent theatre in honour of the town's most famous son. As Stratford's mayor, he opened the Shakespeare Memorial Theatre on Shakespeare's birthday, 23 April 1879. Unfortunately the building was destroyed by fire in 1926, later to be replaced by the Royal Shakespeare Theatre in 1932.

The Dirty Duck is also known as The Black Swan.

DIRTY DUCK
WATERSIDE

He hath a garden circummur'd
    with brick,
Whose western side is with a
    vineyard backd
And to that vineyard is a
    planched gate,
That makes his opening with this
    bigger key;
This other doth command a little
    door,
Which from the vineyard to the
    garden leads.

WILLIAM SHAKESPEARE
Measure for Measure, Act IV, Scene 1
1605

THE OTHER PLACE

Our revels now are ended. These our
    actors,
As I foretold you, were all spirits and
Are melted into air, into thin air:
And, like the baseless fabric of this vision,
The cloud-capped towers, the gorgeous
    palaces,
The solemn temples, the great globe itself,
Yea, all which it inherit, shall dissolve
And, like this insubstantial pageant faded,
Leave not a rack behind. We are such stuff
As dreams are made on, and our little life
Is rounded with a sleep.

WILLIAM SHAKESPEARE
The Tempest, Act IV, Scene 1
1611

RIVER AVON AND HOLY TRINITY CHURCH

… a large and venerable
pile, mouldering with age,
but richly ornamented …
the river runs murmuring
at the foot of the
churchyard, and the elms
which grow upon its banks
droop their branches into
its clear bosom. An avenue
of limes, the boughs of
which are curiously
interlaced, so as to form in
summer an arched way of
foliage, leads up from the
gate of the yard to the
church porch.

WASHINGTON IRVING
The Sketch Book
1848

HOLY TRINITY CHURCH

The aspect of the edifice, as we approached it, was venerable and beautiful, with a great green shadow of trees about it, and the Gothic architecture and vast arched windows obscurely seen above and among the boughs.

<small>NATHANIEL HAWTHORNE
The English Notebooks
27 June 1855</small>

… we saw the monument of old Shakespeare, the famous poet, and whose dramatic features so justly maintain his character among the British poets; and perhaps will do so to the end of time. The busto of his head is in the wall on the north side of the church, and a flat gravestone covers the body, in the isle just under him. On which gravestone these lines are written:

Good frend for Jesus sake
    forbeare
To digg the dust encloased heare
Blessed be ye man yt spares thes
    stones
And curst be he yt moves my
    bones.

<small>DANIEL DEFOE
A Tour through the Whole Island of Great Britain
1724–1726</small>

RIVER AVON

Under the greenwood
    tree
Who loves to lie with
    me,
And turn his merry note
Unto the sweet bird's
    throat,
Come hither, come
    hither, come hither.
Here we shall see
No enemy
But winter and rough
    weather.

WILLIAM SHAKESPEARE
As You Like It, Act II, Scene 5
1600

RIVER AVON AND **WITTER LOCKS**

My route for part of the way lay in sight of the Avon, which made a variety of the most fanciful doublings and windings through a wide and fertile valley; sometimes glittering from among willows, which fringed its borders; sometimes disappearing among groves, or beneath green banks; and sometimes rambling out into full view, and making an azure sweep round a slope of meadow land.

WASHINGTON IRVING
The Sketch Book
1848

HALL'S CROFT

Hall's Croft is probably Stratford's finest
surviving Tudor house. Built on a stone
foundation with oak-timber framing, lath
and plaster, it features a tiled, gabled roof
topped with picturesque chimney stacks.
It was the home of Shakespeare's daughter,
Susanna, and her husband Dr John Hall,
and is furnished in the style of a middle-
class Tudor home of the period.

I know a bank where the wild thyme blows,
Where oxlips and the nodding violet grows,
Quite over-canopied with luscious
    woodbine,
With sweet musk-roses, and with eglantine.
There sleeps Titania, sometime of the night,
Lull'd in these flowers with dances and
    delight.

WILLIAM SHAKESPEARE
A Midsummer Night's Dream, Act 2,
Scene 1
1596

HALL'S CROFT

As the name 'croft' suggests, the garden at
Hall's Croft was once a spacious plot
attached to the house including herb, flower
and kitchen gardens, and an orchard. Today
it comprises an impressive walled garden
with an aged mulberry tree, a herbaceous
border and herb garden.

When Learning's triumph o'er her barb'rous
    foes
First reached the stage, immortal Shakespeare
    rose;
Each change of many-coloured life he drew,
Exhausted worlds, and then imagined new;
Existence saw him spurn her bounded reign,
And panting Time toiled after him in vain.
His pow'rful strokes presiding truth impressed,
And unresisted passion stormed the breast.

SAMUEL JOHNSON
*Prologue spoken by Mr Garrick at the opening of the Theatre
Royal, Drury Lane*
1747

HALL'S CROFT
CONSULTING ROOM

Dr John Hall was a respected physician whose casebook throws considerable light on contemporary medical practice. Published in 1657, it contained 'Select observations on English bodies, or cures both empirical and historical, performed upon very eminent persons in desperate diseases.'

HALL'S CROFT
SERVANT'S BEDCHAMBER

Sleep that knits up the ravell'd sleave of care,
The death of each day's life, sore labour's bath,
Balm of hurt minds, great nature's second
    course,
Chief nourisher in life's feast.

WILLIAM SHAKESPEARE
Macbeth Act II, Scene 2
1606

ALMSHOUSES
CHURCH STREET

There is an almshouse for ten paupers on the south side of Trinity Chapel, which is maintained by a fraternity of the Holy Cross.

JOHN LELAND
John Leland's Itinerary
*c.*1540

The almshouses adjoining the Guild Hall were built in about 1427. They continue to fulfil their original purpose of providing homes for aged local people. The tall brick chimney-stacks above the almshouses were designed to carry sparks well away from the roofs which were originally thatched.

WINDMILL INN
Church Street

The name Stratford means 'ford on the stratum', or Roman road. This road joined the Roman settlements at Alcester and Tiddington, east of Stratford, and the ford was probably near the point where Bridgefoot crosses the Avon now. The town was recorded as 'Stretford' in the eighth century, and as 'Stradforde' in the Domesday Book of 1086.

The web of our life is of a mingled yarn,
good and ill together:
our virtues would not be proud
if our faults whipped them not;
and our crimes would despair
if they were not cherished by our
    virtues.

William Shakespeare
All's Well That Ends Well, Act IV, Scene 3
1603

CHURCH STREET
Grammar School

There is no more interesting school in the county than that to which Shakespeare owed his 'little Latin and less Greek' … in which he learnt and in which Stratford youth had learnt before when as yet there were no scholars at Eton. For the original foundation deed of this 'Free Grammar School of King Edward VI' goes back to 1482, but there is evidence of its existence at a much earlier period.

The Victoria History of the County of Warwick
1908

CHAPEL STREET
Shakespeare Hotel

Following its restoration in the 1860s, Shakespeare's Birthplace attracted a growing number of visitors. Hotels were built to meet demand, including the Red Horse in Bridge Street – mentioned by Washington Irving in his *Sketch Book*, 1848, and now a branch of Marks & Spencers – and the Shakespeare Hotel in Chapel Street.

NASH'S HOUSE

Nash's House belonged to Thomas Nash, a local lawyer and the first husband of Shakespeare's granddaughter, Elizabeth Hall. Its interiors vividly evoke domestic life in Shakespeare's day and there are some fine specimens of Tudor and Jacobean furnishings. It also serves as Stratford's local history museum, illustrating interesting facets of the town's past.

SITE OF NEW PLACE

The original house built by Hugh Clopton at New Place was a large, half-timbered structure, with a courtyard, barns and spacious gardens. Shakespeare bought the property in 1597 for £60 and lived there from 1610 until his death in 1616. The house was pulled down in 1759 by a later owner, the Reverend Francis Gastrell, after a quarrel with the town authorities. Today only the foundations remain.

NASH'S HOUSE
The Parlour

… enrichers of the fancy, strengtheners of virtue, a withdrawing from all selfish and mercenary thoughts, a lesson of all sweet and honourable thoughts and actions, to teach courtesy, benignity, generosity, humanity; for of examples, teaching these virtues, [Shakespeare's] pages are full.

CHARLES AND MARY LAMB
From the preface to *Tales from Shakespeare*
1807

NASH'S HOUSE
Tapestry

Scorn not the Sonnet; Critic, you have frowned,
Mindless of its just honours; with this key
Shakespeare unlocked his heart.

WILLIAM WORDSWORTH
From *Scorn not the Sonnet*
1827

NEW PLACE
KNOT GARDEN

The Knot Garden is an exact replica of the type of enclosed Elizabethan garden that would have been attached to any house of importance in Shakespeare's time. The four 'knots' or beds, divided by stone paths, comprise an intricate mosaic of box, savory, hyssop, cotton lavender, thyme and other traditional herbs.

NEW PLACE
GREAT GARDEN

Now carefully maintained by the Shakespeare Birthplace Trust, the Great Garden comprises the original orchard and kitchen garden of New Place. The long borders between box and yew hedges have been fashioned in the formal manner of Tudor times. There is also a bank of wildflowers and herbs, including savory, hyssop and thyme.

GUILD CHAPEL

Near the south end of the town in a fine street there is an excellent chapel of the Trinity. It was built anew within living memory by one Hugh Clopton, Mayor of London. This Clopton also built an attractive house of brick and timber by the north side of this chapel, where he spent his last years and died.

JOHN LELAND
John Leland's Itinerary
*c.*1540
The house built by Hugh Clopton was New Place, which was demolished in 1579.

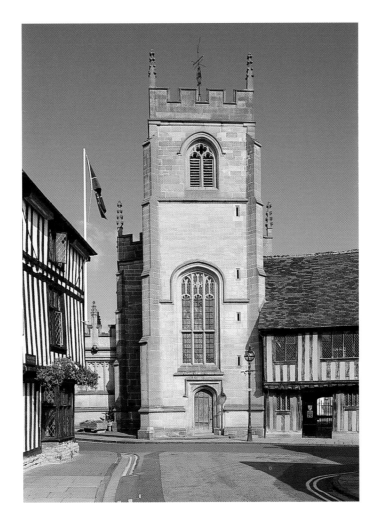

GUILD CHAPEL

The Guild Chapel was built by the influential Guild of the Holy Cross – an association of leading townsmen – in 1269. It was largely rebuilt in the fifteenth century, including the nave and west tower. The latter was provided by Sir Hugh Clopton, a successful Stratford merchant who became Lord Mayor of London and bestowed his wealth on his native town.

ANNE HATHAWAY'S COTTAGE

When Shakespeare's thoughts did lightly turn to love, pleasant were the paths that conducted him to Shottery, the home of Anne Hathaway! Time has dealt leniently with this old world village, and probably were he to revisit the scenes of his life, he would be far more likely to recognise Shottery than Stratford …

CHARLES SHOWELL
Shakespeare's Avon from Source to Severn
1901

BROOK WALK
SHOTTERY

Shottery is a hamlet within the parish of Stratford, just over a mile from the town centre. Although much of the land in between is now built over, in Shakespeare's day it would have been a distinct settlement, separated from Stratford by open fields.

ORCHARD
ANNE HATHAWAY'S COTTAGE

By the standards of Shakespeare's day, Anne Hathaway's 'cottage' was actually the substantial residence of a well-to-do yeoman farmer. It was the childhood home of Shakespeare's wife, Anne. On his death her father bequeathed her £6 13s 4d 'atte the day of her maryage'. She married William Shakespeare in November 1582.

ANNE HATHAWAY'S COTTAGE

The central portion consists of one room containing furniture more or less of a period contemporaneous with him, and very quaint and comfortable it looks ... In the room above is an ancient wooden bedstead, its head divided into panels richly carved; the canopy is supported at the foot by two massive pillars, also richly embellished with carvings. Many other quaint nooks and corners here are worth exploring.

CHARLES SHOWELL
Shakespeare's Avon from Source to Severn
1901

In his will of 25 March 1616, Shakespeare bequeathed his property to the male heirs of his elder daughter, Susanna. To his wife, Anne, he left his 'second-best bed.'

PALMER'S FARM

I constantly carry in my greatcoat pocket the Shakespeare you bought for me in Liverpool. What an unspeakable source of delight that book is to me!

<small>CHARLES DICKENS</small>
Letter from America
22 March 1842

PALMER'S FARM

Shall I compare these to a
    summer's day?
Thou are more lovely and more
    temperate:
Rough winds do shake the
    darling buds of May,
And summer's lease hath all too
    short a date.

<small>WILLIAM SHAKESPEARE</small>
Sonnet XVIII
*c.*1593-99

PALMER'S FARM
Kitchen

Wonderful women! Have you ever thought how much we all, and women especially, owe to Shakespeare for his vindication of women in these fearless, high-spirited, resolute and intelligent heroines?

Dame Ellen Terry (actress)
Four Lectures on Shakespeare
1940

PALMER'S FARM
Wooden Panel

Shakespeare one gets acquainted with without knowing how. It is part of an Englishman's constitution. His thoughts and beauties are so spread abroad that one touches them everywhere, one is intimate with him by instinct.

Jane Austen
Mansfield Park
1814

PALMER'S FARM
HAYRICK

O God! Methinks it were a happy
    life,
To be no better than a homely
    swain;
To sit upon a hill, as I do now,
To carve out dials, quaintly, point
    by point,
Thereby to see the minutes how
    they run,
How many make the hour full
    complete;
How many hours bring about the
    day;
How many days will finish up the
    year;
How many years a mortal man
    may live.

WILLIAM SHAKESPEARE
King Henry the Sixth Part III, Act II, Scene 5
1592

MARY ARDEN'S HOUSE

What a world could I present to
you out of … William
Shakespeare, and other most
pregnant wits of these our times,
whom succeeding ages may justly
admire.

WILLIAM CAMDEN
Remaines of a Greater Worke Concerning Britaine
1605

MARY ARDEN'S HOUSE

This fine timber-framed farmhouse in Wilmcote was named after Shakespeare's mother in the eighteenth century. Until Glebe Farm was identified as her actual home in 2000, it was thought that Palmer's Farm was where Mary Arden lived before she married John Shakespeare and moved to Stratford. The house dates mainly from the sixteenth century. Its central section – a two-bay hall – was originally open to the roof, but a floor was inserted later to create two extra chambers on the first floor.

I could not but reflect on the singular gift of the poet; to be able thus to spread the magic of his mind over the very face of nature; to give to things and places a charm and character not their own, and to turn this 'working-day world' into a perfect fairy land. He is, indeed, the true enchanter, whose spell operates, not upon the senses, but upon the imagination of the heart.

Washington Irving *The Sketch Book* 1848

ASTON CANTLOW CHURCH

… this fine church to which one day Mary Arden came from Wilmcote and John Shakespeare from Snitterfield for that union of hearts which was to give the world its greatest Englishman.

ARTHUR MEE
The King's England: Warwickshire
1936

ASTON CANTLOW

Indeed the whole country about here is poetic ground; every thing is associated with the idea of Shakspeare. Every old cottage that I saw I fancied into some resort of his boyhood, where he had acquired his intimate knowledge of rustic life and manners …

WASHINGTON IRVING
The Sketch Book
1848

COUGHTON COURT
VIEW OF ST PETER'S CHURCH AND THE GATEHOUSE

Now in the property of the National Trust, this historic family mansion lies 10 miles from Stratford in the Vale of Arrow. Coughton belonged to the Catholic family of Throckmorton from the fifteenth century, and was one of the haunts frequented by the conspirators responsible for the Gunpowder Plot of 1605. Vehicles and horses originally passed through Coughton's imposing gateway, one of the finest examples of its class in England. It features the arms of Henry VIII on its upper oriel. Coughton's extensive landscaped grounds contain a lake and riverside walks.

COUGHTON COURT
ROOF VIEW

There are extensive views of the Shakespeare Country from the roof at Coughton Court, with flat ground to the west and a more varied landscape across the River Arrow to the east. The fashion for taking visitors on roof walks of houses was waning by the end of the seventeenth century, but in its heyday this vantage point would have provided a perfect position for watching sporting activities in the grounds.

COUGHTON COURT
ENTRANCE HALL

Looking out over the courtyard from inside the 'stately castle-like Gate-house of freestone', as it was described by Dugdale, the seventeenth-century Warwickshire historian.

HENLEY-IN-ARDEN

Nowhere in Warwickshire shall we find a street more varied in timbered walls and crazy roofs, in ancient windows and hoary gables, in doors and doorways so gracefully grown old. Along these pavements we step into Tudor England … a museum of domestic architecture.

ARTHUR MEE
The King's England: Warwickshire
1936

MARKET CROSS
HENLEY-IN-ARDEN

O Rosalind! These trees shall be my books
And in their barks my thoughts I'll character;
That every eye which in this forest looks
Shall see thy virtue witness'd every where.
Run, run, Orlando; carve on every tree
The fair, the chaste and unexpressive she.

WILLIAM SHAKESPEARE
As You Like It, Act III, Scene 2
1600
The setting for this play is the Forest of Arden.

PACKWOOD HOUSE

Tucked away among the country lanes between Lapworth and Knowle is Packwood House, given to the National Trust in 1941 by Graham Baron Ash. It dates from Tudor times but has been extensively restored and enlarged. Inside, its rooms are furnished with fine tapestries, period furniture and Jacobean panelling.

PACKWOOD HOUSE

We must count [the yews] as the great and proud achievement of an English garden. They are a mighty host, rank on rank, large and small, all perfectly trimmed and seeming to hold in their green depths the solemnity of the ages. They are Nature's monuments to the patience of man.

ARTHUR MEE
The King's England: Warwickshire
1936

BADDESLEY CLINTON

As gracious a house as we could wish to find in Old England, it has venerable walls and an embattled gate-tower with all the charm the Tudor builders could give them, mullioned windows, timbered gables, and tall brick chimneys.

ARTHUR MEE
The King's England: Warwickshire
1936

KENILWORTH CASTLE

The Gentlemen carried no arms, save their swords and daggers. These gallants were as gaily dressed as imagination could devise, and as the garb of the time permitted a great display of expensive magnificence, nought was to be seen but velvet and cloth of gold and silver, ribands, feathers, gems and golden chains.

Sir Walter Scott
Kenilworth
1821

Of the numerous castles of England Kenilworth is undoubtedly one of the grandest. It has superb Norman, C14, and Elizabethan work, and where … one sees all three together and all three in the strong yet mellow red of their sandstone, the view could not be bettered.

Nikolaus Pevsner and Alexandra Wedgwood
The Buildings of England: Warwickshire
1966

ROYAL LEAMINGTON SPA
Jephson Gardens

The Jephson Gardens are the floral crown of the town … shady walks by the River Leam, with their broad lawns, their spacious flower beds, their terraced rockeries, their rosaries, and the fountains copied from Hampton Court. In these gardens stands the bronze statue of Dr Jephson, who brought much fame to Leamington by the use of its spa waters.

Arthur Mee
The King's England: Warwickshire
1936

ROYAL LEAMINGTON SPA
Lansdowne Crescent

'Genteel' is the word for it … the tasteful shop-fronts on the principal streets; the Bath-chairs; the public gardens; the servants whom one meets, and doubts whether they are groom, footman, or butler, or a mixture of the three; the ladies sweeping through the avenues; the nursery maids and children … I do not know a spot where I would rather reside than in this new village of midmost Old England.

Nathaniel Hawthorne *The English Notebooks* 10 September 1857

WARWICK
LORD LEYCESTER HOSPITAL

An ancient edifice, in excellent repair, and with the coats of arms and the cognizance of the Bear and Ragged Staff painted on its front. This turns out to be Leicester's Hospital, an institution for the support of twelve poor brethren …

NATHANIEL HAWTHORNE
The English Notebooks
27 June 1855

WARWICK
LORD LEYCESTER HOPSITAL

I presume there is nothing else so perfect in England, in this style and date of architecture, as this interior quadrangle of Leicester's Hospital … the twelve brethren are selected from among men of good character, who have been in military service, and, by preference, natives of Warwickshire or Gloucestershire. [They] receive from the Hospital an annuity of eighty pounds each, besides their apartments, a garment of fine blue cloth, with a silver badge, an annual quantity of ale, and a right at the kitchen fire.

NATHANIEL HAWTHORNE
The English Notebooks
30 October 1857

WARWICK CASTLE

Whether we see it from the bridge with the Avon flowing beneath it, or walk along the winding way cut for 100 yards through solid rock and stand entranced by this vast place across the lawns, we feel that we are looking down the corridor of time through English history … These walls have seen something of the splendour of every generation of our story since Richard Beauchamp entertained Henry of Agincourt here.

ARTHUR MEE
The King's England: Warwickshire
1936

This magnificent feudal fortress … designed more as an exuberant display of the power of the Beauchamp family than as a functional fighting machine.

GEOFFREY TYACK AND STEVEN BUNDELL
Blue Guide: Country Houses of England
1994

103

WARWICK CASTLE

The English, it is plain, are fond of travelling, and make the pleasure last as long as they can. Gentlemen's grounds, mansions, and genteel cottages, numerous everywhere, seem more so here than ever … a fine fruitful country – avenues of giant elms – large oaks and ash …

LOUIS SIMOND
An American in Regency England: the journal of a tour in 1810-1811

Formerly the home of the Earl of Warwick, whose ancestors had such an impact on the course of medieval history (Richard Neville, 'Warwick the King Maker', lived here from 1449 to 1471), Warwick Castle is a treasure house of architectural and artistic interest. Inside it is magnificently furnished, and contains an oubliette or dungeon within a dungeon, the famous portrait of Elizabeth I in her coronation robes, and a collection of armour including pieces worn by the Black Prince.

CHARLECOTE PARK

Charlecote has been the home of the Lucy family for over 700 years. Its mellow brickwork and great chimneys capture the very essence of Tudor England. The deer park, with its Shakespearian associations, was later landscaped by 'Capability' Brown.

[Charlecote Park] is bounded by the peculiarly picturesque irregular wooden fence so frequently seen round a deer park. Inside may be seen fine antlered deer, browsing under gigantic elms, which seem to be characteristic of the place …

CHARLES SHOWELL
Shakespeare's Avon from Source to Severn
1901

HIDCOTE MANOR

American-born Lawrence Johnston created the gardens at Hidcote Manor piece by piece from adjoining farmland. The result is perhaps England's most influential twentieth-century garden, with a dazzling patchwork of 'rooms', each different in mood, with changes in scale, design and colour at each turn.

HIDCOTE MANOR

Hidcote Manor was the first property that the National Trust acquired specifically for its garden. For the planting Lawrence Johnston consulted garden designer Norah Lindsay and the plants are carefully positioned according to colour, texture and flowering season.

HIDCOTE MANOR

Where the bee sucks, there suck I:
In a cowslip's bell I lie;
There I couch when owls do cry.
On the bat's back I do fly
After summer merrily.
Merrily, merrily I shall live now
Under the blossom that hangs on
    the bough.

WILLIAM SHAKESPEARE
The Tempest, Act V, Scene 1
1611

HIDCOTE BARTRIM

For so work the honey bees,
Creatures that by a rule in nature teach
The act of order to a peopled kingdom.
They have a king and officers of sorts:
Where some like magistrates correct at home,
Others like merchants venture trade abroad;
Others like soldiers armed in their stings
Make boot upon the summer's velvet buds.

WILLIAM SHAKESPEARE
King Henry V, Act I, Scene 2
1599

VALE OF EVESHAM

As the River Avon enters the Vale of Evesham
the landscape subtly alters. Arable fields give
way to orchards, fruit farms and market
gardens. The area is a centre for fruit and
vegetable growing, and in spring the vale is
carpeted with fruit blossom. Much of this
part of rural England was formerly covered
by the Forest of Arden.

EVESHAM ABBEY

Evesham was named after Eoves, a swineherd for Egwin, the Bishop of Worcester, in the eighth century. Eoves had a vision of the Virgin Mary which convinced the bishop, later to become St Egwin, that a monastery should be founded here. Today only a Norman gateway and a fifteenth-century Bell Tower remain.

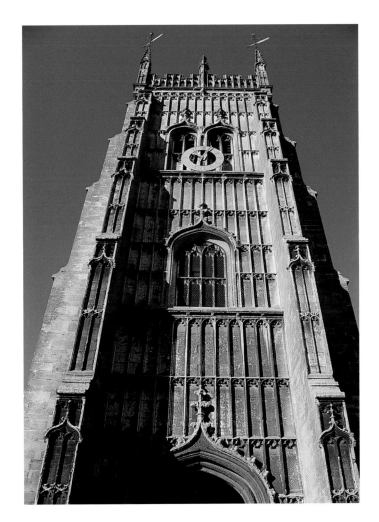

EVESHAM ABBEY

Passing between the churches, we are confronted with Evesham's glory – its Bell Tower. Between this tower and the river were the Abbey buildings – with one or two exceptions the most extensive in England. Alas! They are all swept away by the baneful hand of that questionable reformer, Henry VIII. Why could he not have left such beautiful buildings to be admired and loved, yea, reverenced, by countless ages unborn?

CHARLES SHOWELL
Shakespeare's Avon from Source to Severn
1901

BIDFORD-ON-AVON

Here the charm of the river is almost at its best and it can have changed little since [Shakespeare] saw it. All about us here is the countryside he knew, the placid flowing river, the bridges and the hamlets, the green meadows and pastures and still waters of his own homeland.

ARTHUR MEE
The King's England: Warwickshire
1936

WELFORD-ON-AVON

… under an American sun (that is to say, once or twice a year) nothing more could be asked by mortals, in the way of rural beauty. All along the way, there were cottages of old date, many so old that Shakespeare might have passed them in his walks, or entered their low doors.

NATHANIEL HAWTHORNE
The English Notebooks
27 June 1855

RAGLEY HALL

That time of year thou may'st in me
 behold,
When yellow leaves, or none, or few,
 do hang
Upon those boughs which shake
 against the cold, –
Bare ruin'd choirs, where late the sweet
 birds sang.

WILLIAM SHAKESPEARE
Sonnet LXXIII
*c.*1593–99

Ragley Hall has been the family home
of the Hertford (Conway Seymour)
family since it was built in 1680. It
features elegant Baroque plasterwork
and a hall described by Horace
Walpole as 'leviathan' – the last major
work of James Gibbs. There is also a
series of *trompe l'oeil* murals called
'Temptation', painted by Graham Rust
between 1969 and 1981.

Acknowledgements

Every effort has been made to secure permissions from copyright owners to use the extracts of text featured in this book.

Any subsequent correspondence should be sent to Jarrold Publishing at the following address:
Jarrold Publishing, Whitefriars, Norwich NR3 1TR

page

12 (left) From *John Leland's Itinerary*, edited by John Chandler. Sutton Publishing, 1998. Reproduced by kind permission of the publishers.

12 (right) From *The Buildings of England: Warwickshire* by Nikolaus Pevsner and Alexandra Wedgwood. Penguin Books, 1990.

16 From *The Sketch Book* by Washington Irving, 1848. G Bell & Sons, Ltd, 1912.

19 (top) From *The English Notebooks* (Vols XXI, XXII) by Nathaniel Hawthorne, edited by Thomas Woodson and Bill Ellis. Reproduced by permission of Ohio State University Press, 1997.

19 (bottom) From *Aubrey's Brief Lives* edited by Oliver Lawson Dick. Publshe by Secker & Warburg. Used by permission of the Random House Group Limited.

24 (left) From *The Adventures of Huckleberry Finn* by Mark Twain. Camden Classics.

24 (right) From *The Critical Opinions of John Dryden*, compiled and edited by John Aden. Used by permission of the Vanderbilt University Press, 1963. Copyright John M. Aden.

27 (left) From *The Rivers and Streams of England* by A.G. Bradley. Adam & Charles Black, 1909. Reprinted 1993, Bracken Books.

28 (right) From *The Buildings of England: Warwickshire* by Nikolaus Pevsner and Alexandra Wedgwood. Penguin Books, 1990.

31 (right) From *The Rivers and Streams of England* by A.G. Bradley. Adam & Charles Black, 1909. Reprinted 1993, Bracken Books.

32 (left) From *The Rivers and Streams of England* by A.G. Bradley. Adam & Charles Black, 1909. Reprinted 1993, Bracken Books.

32 (right) From *John Leland's Itinerary*, edited by John Chandler. Sutton Publishing, 1998. Reproduced by kind permission of the publishers.

34 (left) From *The Life of Samuel Johnson* by James Boswell, edited by Christopher Hibbert. Penguin, 1986.

34 (right) From *The Buildings of England: Warwickshire* by Nikolaus Pevsner and Alexandra Wedgwood. Penguin Books, 1990.

37 (top) From *Garrick* by John McIntyre. Allen Lane, 1999.

37 (bottom) From *The Illustrated Pepys* edited by Robert Latham. Penguin, 2000.

38 (right) From *The Victoria History of the County of Warwick* (Volume

Old Town, Stratford-upon-Avon

II), edited by W. Page. Published by Constable and Company, 1908.

41 (right) From *The Sketch Book* by Washington Irving, 1848. G Bell & Sons, Ltd, 1912.

44 (right) From *The Sketch Book* by Washington Irving, 1848. G Bell & Sons, Ltd, 1912.

47 (left) From *The English Notebooks* (Vols XXI, XXII) by Nathaniel Hawthorne, edited by Thomas Woodson and Bill Ellis. Reproduced by permission of Ohio State University Press, 1997.

48 (bottom) From *The Sketch Book* by Washington Irving, 1848. G Bell & Sons, Ltd, 1912.

52 (bottom) From *Samuel Johnson*, edited by Donald Green. OUP, 1984.

57 (top) From *John Leland's Itinerary*, edited by John Chandler. Sutton Publishing, 1998. Reproduced by kind permission of the publishers.

65 (left) From the preface to *Tales from Shakespeare* by Charles and Mary Lamb. Paul Hamlyn, 1966.

65 (right) From *Wordsworth's Poetical Works*, edited by Thomas Hutchinson, 1904, revised by E. de Selincourt. Oxford University Press, 1936.

69 (left) From *John Leland's Itinerary*,

edited by John Chandler. Sutton Publishing, 1998. Reproduced by kind permission of the publishers.

70 From *Shakespeare's Avon from Source to Severn* by Charles Showell. Cornish Brothers, 1901.

75 From *Shakespeare's Avon from Source to Severn* by Charles Showell. Cornish Brothers, 1901.

76 (left) From *The Life of Charles Dickens* by John Forster. Published by Cecil Palmer, 1928.

79 (left) From *Bloomsbury Thematic Dictionary of Quotations*, edited by John Daintith. Published by Bloomsbury 1988. Reproduced by permission of Bloomsbury Publishing plc.

79 (right) From *Mansfield Park* by Jane Austen. Reproduced by permission of Penguin.

83 (right) From *The Sketch Book* by Washington Irving, 1848. G Bell & Sons, Ltd, 1912.

84 (left) *From *The King's England: Warwickshire* by Arthur Mee. Used by kind permission of The King's England Press Ltd.

84 (right) From *The Sketch Book* by Washington Irving, 1848. G Bell & Sons, Ltd, 1912.

90 (top) From *The King's England: Warwickshire* by Arthur Mee. Used

by kind permission of The King's England Press Ltd.

94 From *The King's England: Warwickshire* by Arthur Mee. Used by kind permission of The King's England Press Ltd.

96 (top) From *Kenilworth* by Sir Walter Scott. J M Dent, 1958.

96 (bottom) From *The Buildings of England: Warwickshire* by Nikolaus Pevsner and Alexandra Wedgwood. Penguin Books, 1990.

99 (left) From *The King's England: Warwickshire* by Arthur Mee. Used by kind permission of The King's England Press Ltd.

99 (right) From *The English Notebooks* (Vols XXI, XXII) by Nathaniel Hawthorne, edited by Thomas Woodson and Bill Ellis. Reproduced by kind permission of Ohio State University Press, 1997.

100 From *The English Notebooks* (Vols XXI, XXII) by Nathaniel Hawthorne, edited by Thomas Woodson and Bill Ellis. Reproduced by permission of Ohio State University Press, 1997.

103 (top) From *The King's England: Warwickshire* by Arthur Mee. Used by kind permission of The King's England Press Ltd.

103 (bottom) From *Blue Guide: Country Houses of England* by Geoffrey Tyack and Steven Bundell. A & C Black, 1994.

104 (top) From *An American in Regency England: the journal of a tour in 1810-1811* by Louis Simond, edited by Christopher Hibbert. Published Pergamon Press, 1968.

107 (bottom) From *Shakespeare's Avon from Source to Severn* by Charles Showell. Cornish Brothers, 1901.

115 (right) From *Shakespeare's Avon from Source to Severn* by Charles Showell. Cornish Brothers, 1901.

116 (top) From *The King's England: Warwickshire* by Arthur Mee. Used by kind permission of The King's England Press Ltd.

116 (bottom) From *The English Notebooks* (Vols XXI, XXII) by Nathaniel Hawthorne, edited by Thomas Woodson and Bill Ellis. Reproduced by permission of Ohio State University Press, 1997.

*The King's England Press is currently reprinting all of Arthur Mee's *King's England* county guidebooks in a facsimile of the original 1936–1953 editions.

Bibliography

Editions and dates in this bibliography are those of the items that have been examined. In some cases earlier editions have significant differences to those listed here.

Austen, Jane: *Mansfield Park*. First published 1814. Published in reissued edition by Penguin, 1986.

Bloomsbury Thematic Dictionary of Quotations, edited by John Daintith. Published by Bloomsbury, 1988.

Boswell, James: *The Life of Samuel Johnson*, edited by Christopher Hibbert. Penguin 1986.

Bradley, A.G.: *The Rivers and Streams of England*. Adam & Charles Black, 1909. Reprinted 1993, Bracken Books.

Burgess, Alan: *Warwickshire*. Robert Hale, 1950.

Chamberlin, Russell: *The English Country Town*. (The National Trust) Webb & Bowes, Exeter, 1983.

de Selincourt, E. (ed): *Wordsworth's Poetical Works*. OUP, 1936.

Campbell, Oscar James (ed): *A Shakespeare Encyclopaedia*. Methuen 1966.

Chambers, E.K.: *William Shakespeare: A study of facts and problems* (Vols I & II). OUP, 1963.

Dodd, Arthur H.: *Life in Elizabethan England*. Batsford, 1964.

Forster, John: T*he Life of Charles Dickens*. Cecil Palmer, 1928.

Fowler, Alastair: *The New Oxford Book of Seventeenth Century Verse*. OUP, 1991.

Fox, Levi: *Historic Stratford-upon-Avon*. Jarrold Publishing 1986. Last reprinted 1999.

Fox, Levi: *Shakespeare's Town & Country*. Jarrold Publishing 1986. Last reprinted 1996.

Fox, Levi: *Stratford-upon-Avon and the Shakespeare Country*. Jarrold Publishing, 1988. Last reprinted 1999.

Country Artists' Fountain, Bancroft Gardens

Fox, Levi: *The Stratford Shakespeare Anthology.* Jarrold Publishing 1996.

Green, Donald (ed): *Samuel Johnson.* OUP, 1984.

Halliday, F.E.: *A Shakespeare Companion.* Gerald Duckworth & Co, 1952.

Hawthorne, Nathaniel: *The English Notebooks* (Vols XXI, XXII), edited by Thomas Woodson and Bill Ellis. Ohio State University Press, 1997.

Irving, Washington: *The Sketch Book* by 1848. G Bell & Sons, Ltd, 1912.

Lamb, Charles and Mary: *Tales from Shakespeare.* Paul Hamlyn, 1966.

Lambert, D.H. (ed): *Shakespeare Documents.* George Bell and Sons, 1904.

Latham, Robert (ed): *The Illustrated Pepys.* Penguin, 2000.

Leland, John: *Leland's Itinerary,* edited by John Chandler. Alan Sutton Publishing, 1993.

McIntyre, John: *Garrick.* Allen Lane, 1999

Mee, Arthur: *The King's England: Warwickshire.* The King's England Press, 1991.

Page, W. (ed): *The Victoria History of the County of Warwick* (Volume II). Constable and Company, 1908.

Pearson, Lu E.: *Elizabethans at Home.* Stanford University Press, 1957.

Room, Adrian: *A Dictionary of Place Names.* Bloomsbury Publishing, 1993.

Scott, Sir Walter: *Kenilworth.* J.M. Dent, 1958.

Shakespeare, William: *The Complete Works of Shakespeare.* HarperCollins, 1994.

Showell, Charles: *Shakespeare's Avon from Source to Severn.* Cornish Brothers, 1901.

Simond, Louis: *An American in Regency England,* edited by Christopher Hibbert. Robert Maxwell, 1968.

Sitwell, Sacheverell: *Sacheverell Sitwell's England,* edited by Michael Raeburn. Little, Brown & Co, 1986.

St Clare Byrne, Muriel: *Elizabethan Life in Town and Country,* 4th ed. Methuen, 1906.

Talbot, Rob and Whiteman, Robin: *Shakespeare's Avon: A Journey from Source to Severn.* Viking, 1989.

Twain, Mark: *The Adventures of Huckleberry Finn.* Camden Classics.

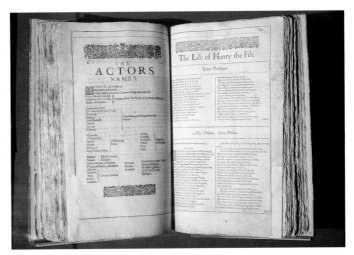

An edition of Shakespeare's plays, The Shakespeare Centre

The Parlour, Shakespeare's Birthplace

Index

GROUNDCOVER
SERIES